Jeannette Harris
My Poppa J is a girl

All rights reserved
Copyright © 2024 by **Jeannette Harris**

Published by Spines
ISBN: 979-8-89569-638-5

"I want to dedicate this book to:
Anthony, Taylor, Peyton, Ayden, Noreno,
Ava, Whoody, Gianna, Grace.
And to all the rest of you, I'll be Your Poppa J
too!"

My poppa J is a girl.

Still she does anything a poppa
would DO!

She takes us fishing,
gives us piggy back rides
and sometimes,
acts like a monster TOO!

SHE TAKES US CAMPING
AND TELLS US STORIES!

SHE PROTECTS US
FROM THE SCARY THINGS

SO WE NEVER
HAVE TO WORRY!

We get the best puzzles and toys

SHE PLAYS WITH US,
TICKLES OUR FEET,

FILLS US
WITH
SO MUCH
JOY!

ONE YEAR SHE THREW US A PARTY
FOR VALENTINES DAY!

BECAUSE WE ARE THE LOVES
OF HER LIFE, AND IT WILL
ALWAYS BE THAT WAY.

SHE READS TO US,
WE WATCH MOVIES
WITH POPCORN.

We take walks in the PARK,
where her dogs
love to BARK!

MY POPPA J ISN'T PERFECT.
THEN AGAIN....
NO ONE REALLY IS.

BUT BECAUSE OF THE LOVE
SHE HAS FOR US,
WE´RE HAPPY
SHE IS WHO SHE IS.

MY POPPA J IS A GIRL!
ALTHOUGH I NEVER UNDERSTOOD HOW.

SHE DOESNT WEAR
CURLS OR PEARLS
OR ANYTHING MEANT FOR GIRLS!

My Poppa J

WEARS BOOTS
AND A BIG FLOPPY HAT.

IMANGINE THAT!
SHE WEARS HER HAIR SHORT
AND LOVES ALL SPORTS!

Instead of a grandpa,
we have Poppa J!
She's a girl
and thats ok!

We love everything
about her
and wouldn't change a thing!

WE WOULDN'T TRADE
OUR POPPA J
FOR ANY OTHER POPPA
IN THE WORLD!
SHE'S PERFECT FOR US,
AND I'M GLAD SHE'S A GIRL.

ONE DAY, I'M GONNA BE
JUST LIKE HER

JUST SHOW EVERYONE LOVE
NO MATTER WHO THEY ARE

Jeannette Harris